DEFENDER

DEFENDER

DREW GARDNER

EDGE

ALSO BY THE AUTHOR

Sugar Pill (Krupskaya, 2002)
Petroleum Hat (Roof, 2005)
Chomp Away (Combo, 2010)
Flarf Orchestra (audio CD, Edge Books, 2011)
Flarf: An Anthology of Flarf (co-editor, Edge Books, 2017)
Ingenious Beauty (editor, University of New Mexico Press, 2018)

☆

Some of these poems have appeared in: *Abraham Lincoln, The Awl, Across the Margin, Boog, The Brooklyn Rail, The Claudius App, Coconut, Empty Mirror, The Equalizer, Flarf, An Anthology of Flarf, The Incredible Sestina Anthology, Ladowich, Lemon Hound, Poetry, Postmodern American Poetry: A Norton Anthology, Relentless, Resist Much/Obey Little, Vanitas, Vlak,* and *West Wind Review.*

Cover: Emma Tapley, *Cultivating the Empty Field*, 2016, oil on panel, 24" x 30".
Design and typesetting by Deirdre Kovac.

ISBN: 978-1-890311-47-6

Edge Books are published by Rod Smith, editor of Aerial magazine, and distributed by Small Press Distribution, Berkeley, CA; 1-800-869-7553; www.spdbooks.org.

Edge Books
P.O. Box 25642, Georgetown Station
Washington, D.C. 20027

aerialedge@gmail.com   www.aerialedge.com

CONTENTS

IT'S YOUR BIRTHDAY

and the entire world is illuminated by a single ferret.
Nearness as new as Albert Finney
failing to recognize that life is a Princess Diana
crash inquest unfolding forever
in Michael Bolton's mind.

I have days when I look in the mirror and I'm
humped to death by an evil disembodied head.
Norm, forty-five is a ripe old age for a hunter.

Evidence is monster.
Celebrates like a beetle in its power.
I used to smoke the emperor of ice station zebra,
a somewhat smaller time dilation
created in the middle of cooking dinner
when we were wandering loose in the calendar.

A world of bottomless holes and spelling errors
made by shambling, intelligent plants.
When I laugh I use a piece of information.

She had fifty eyes and the glowing bill of a toucan.

No, I won't get in your car.
You can pass me the ferret
through the window.

BY THE LOOKS OF IT, I'M GETTING STOOD UP

I know it must sound implausible,
but I have a middle-aged friend
who sucks his thumb and I don't know
if I can take it anymore.

Fire sucks.
Fire and earth and air suck.
Your pets are treating you
with a certain care,
skateboarding on those with wigs of words.
I love staring at one-sided figures.

Tell your friends to stop whaling.
Painful Dungeons and Dragons tears
when the library is overwhelmed,
like working with a latex cosmonaut
who makes a shirt into a phone call,
picks mouse hats for nose jobs
based on tiles of mom and dad.
Doing it and dreading it well.

ALL THE WORLD LOVES A BIG GLEAMING JELLY

we read the cake, and ate the poem,
felt spry with days trees dolor more and over
wheel locks with Lojack
in joined hands across my wish
pass the leaf earlier than every growth expected
the sea with the soup
as through pierced ears
an elf-shot heady swagger with frayed nerves wondered
so much helpless groping
of those drawing inspiration
till they felt-up like anyone born at all
familiar as a face in the street,
to walk beyond the sidewalks
the vending machines and cars
organs in the insignificant darkness
in the inside of the body
that jack built for me and you.
I see a postage stamp
that makes up daily life in
sparks that own me
sometimes a green bile monster
sometimes a song, where blows a nematode
white magnolias break into sight

RAISED BY WOLVES

The confusing human world
looks at faces, not feral children
raised by kalimbas.
Romulus and Remus ping United States.
Whose meaning?

His camera brought together
by fears and bitches
equal to us, wrote the pharaoh.
A human child is your boss
surviving the food
born by encyclopedias.

I want my dog to feel equal to human freedom,
but what do these "freedom instructions" mean?
No one should speak
to themselves, but the shepherd should feed
and care for their wolves.
The first word would be uttered
in the root language
of all wolves.

When one of the children cried "because"
(a sound like the bleating of sheep)
with outstretched paws
the word was bread,
the social structure
clear and unambiguous,
and where the primal needs
for exercise, structure, and affection
are met fairly and consistently
by wolves, Egyptian wolves
integrating themselves into the space library.

Some dog lovers protest
when I ask them to step up
and become pack leader.

RUDOLPH THE TRANSCENDENT MINIMALIST WHITE SUPREMACIST RITUAL CHILD ABUSER

Who knows the value of a very shiny monad,
a moment of total clarity, turning in the
lie detector test for amber waves of pain.
If you ever saw him
when time is too busy and years think things through,
you would ask who can think
for an hour without needing a receipt.
Who knows the value of a power that kills millions
who makes experts talk into a palette of rescuing beagles,
to identify all the maybes.
He who is content to share a feeling with friends
used to laugh and know the value of Tituba,
when meaning can draw poor Rudolph
into any reindeer witch trials.
He who is soundly versed in systematic Christmas Eve
when Santas came to say,
with your mind so bright,
you simply trust in a just and loving witch,
won't guide my sleigh
through values or systems
as they shouted out with trees
that he is a creator
who knows the meaning of not saying
anything, and used his credit card.
Maybe you'll go down in history.
Who cares.

SO YOU'RE JUST GONNA STAND THERE AND PICK THE ICING OFF THE CAKE?

Teenage birth rate rises to fuel
the National Endowment for the War,
shifting amid the creation of your parents.
I'm free to give my analysis of the situation,
deals with general computer problems
making it impossible for you to be surprised to learn
that Elvis is popular in Afghanistan.

I feel huffy staring at empty space.
The cryptography is solid, but the generation
of keys isn't working.
Propellers are curvy and symmetrical.

Polishes a new pitcher for the promise of not working.
I don't want to lose weight by loosing fat.
I want to loose everything else and become
a quivering pile of NOTHING BUT FAT.

I remember as a kid my dad played an Ed Meese record for me.
A generation of interventionist, statist landlords
responsible for the creation of the debt-ridden
idea-centered universe when
violence is rising despite a shift
in US military tactics to panda porn
that fails to teach pandas
how to knock each other up.
Is branding dead?

Specializing in energized people
who have forgotten the history lessons
Don Henley has taught us.
It all depends on what you mean by "it's not working."

ON FIRE

Do you smell something burning?
The eye is burning. Imps are on fire in my mind.
I know things. I was in an array.
A kind of recession was happening.
Pleasant or painful, not painful, nor pleasant,
the striking visuals make a scene.
Using stuff up. Consuming.

The smell is burning, particles of matter sent to the brain.
Sending is burning, also whatever sending,
nice or nasty, or neither nice nor nasty,
on account of the sending.

Smoke detectors can alert you to a fire
in time for you to escape, even if you are asleep.
Install smoke detectors on every level.

Feeling like shit in the mind, finds feeling like shit in ideas,
finds feeling like shit for way too long, in contact with people,
and whatever is felt as pleasant or painful or
neither, the arteries and veins send blood
with eye-contact killing yourself off because you've got bigger
and better plans for yourself or putting off
killing yourself off
for its indispensable condition,
like a coal mine fire underground in Pennsylvania.

The Malibu fires were raging.
The skies were red, and smoke had blown east
all the way to Barstow.
I just want to be somewhere.
I want to be with a person. I want to be a kind of person.
I want to do things and have abilities.
Every moment decisions are burning
with the fire of wanting something but not wanting
to make painful decisions.

Testing detectors every month,
following the directions, and replacing batteries is burning.
Whenever a detector "chirps"
to signal a low source of power, respond.
Never borrow a detector's source of power for something else.
A disabled detector can't help you.
Replace detectors that get old.

I started to get old, started becoming a surfer,
and lived in a circus tent.
Was I in love with surfing?
I just want to spend all my time moving
from one side of a wave to the other,
choosing a wave like a blank page or a state of mind,
knowing what is supposed to happen.

Tactile stuff is burning, tactile feeling is
totally burning up for your love.
Whatever sensation, pleasant or painful or neither painful nor pleasant,
arises on account of the tactile stuff, that too is burning.
Burning with the fire of wanting something.
Get out of the room now. . . .

But that's how it is when you're on fire with something.
Everything changes: that it's a cliché doesn't effect its truth value.
The way you look at the fire, and the future,
even your senses are somehow . . . I'd guess a gardenia.
Or looking at stars, they move slowly
and I think, Wow, that is so *you*!
You are moving so slowly like angry music with new meaning.
Peace, love and understanding are burning.
Plan your escape from fire.

Be sure that everyone knows at least two unobstructed escapes.
Doors and windows – they are burning escapes.
Not including elevators in your plan is burning.
Deciding on a meeting place is burning.
Everyone you've ever known
will practice your escape with you. That too is on fire.

The smell of roofing tar,
cold coal cold iron un-melted because
your hand is not hot enough to melt it. Heat is power.
Your hand is like a furnace that can melt chocolate.

Burning with the fire of wanting something, with the fire of hate,
with the fire of delusion – this is burning.
It is burning with life, experience and completion,
with depression, with physical pain, comfort and joy.
It was October and I was sort of speaking in tongues.
I looked out at the people talking to fire
in their various private languages.
I saw light in their eyes, the intensity on their faces and I thought,
Have I become detached? I don't feel free.
My life is confusing, the life I have already
lived seems contained in my mind.
There is no more left to be done on this account.
How did I start on a path of wanting
and end up with a bunch of white people
shouting at each other?

Keeping an eye on smokers is burning.
Smoking in bed or when you are drowsy is burning.
Checking under and around cushions and upholstered furniture
for smoldering cigarettes is burning.
The fire showed me the door.
Have you told yourself how hot you really are?
You should check this out. Blow your own doors off.

You know that bad boyfriend you know you
shouldn't give another chance?
I want what you want to burn I say by burning
and burn by saying I want to know things.
I want fuel.

It was like Slayer was playing.
I remember one song we tranced out to
All Consuming Fire – fuck yeah!
Pulling punches is burning.

The ear is burning. Sounds are burning.
Auditory feeling is on fire, sending information and interpreting it.
Also whatever sensation, whatever striking sounds, whatever interpretation
pleasant or painful or neither painful nor pleasant,
arises on account of the sound impression, that too is burning.

Crawling low is burning.
Smoke and poisonous gases rise with the heat.
Everyone is the same: 98.6 degrees.
The air is cleaner near the floor.
If you encounter smoke while you are escaping from a fire,
use another way.

Who sees things becomes cool with the eye,
becomes cool with visible stuff,
becomes cool with visual consciousness,
becomes cool with visual impression,
also whatever sensation, pleasant or painful or neither painful nor pleasant,
arises on account of the incredible visuals.
Letting people love you? That's your love story.

The tongue is burning. Flavors are burning.
Being full of fuel is burning, taste is burning,
pleasant or painful or neither painful nor pleasant,
arises on account of the mind that controls your digestive track.
Impression is burning.
Burning with the fire of wanting some goddamn food.

Never leave cooking unattended.
Keep cooking areas clear
and wear clothes with short, rolled-up or tight-fitting sleeves.
Turn pot handles inward,
even if you are turned outward.
Leave the lid on until cool.
Like Harry Potter magic.
Like being in a trance, only not as cool.
Become cool with the body, cool with tangible things.
My vacation was officially ruined.

I used some ointment that was supposed to heal me.
It was totally useless.

Give space heaters space,
at least three feet from anything that can burn,
and never leave them on when you leave home or go to bed.
Some life drawing today.
I was on fire. Well, I *think* I was. . . .
I hate not being in class.

I have waited for things.
And I've gone to conferences.
I've been zapped with a taser.
Feeling like shit in the eye,
finds feeling like shit in forms,
finds feeling like shit in ideas,
finds feeling like shit in eye-contact,
and whatever is felt as pleasant or painful or neither
painful nor pleasant that arises with eye-contact
for its indispensable condition,
in that too he acts like a total brat.
Where's that hobby horse my ancestors gave me?
Feeling that you haven't lived is burning.
Feeling you've lived too much is burning.
In a child's hand, matches and lighters can be deadly.
Use only child-resistant lighters and keep matches and lighters
up high, where small children can't see or reach them.

I love the stars burning with a burning love in the sky.
Getting a real job is burning. I want to work for them.
On fire in the unemployment line, unemployment is burning.
Run cool water over a burn for ten to fifteen minutes.
Never put butter or any grease on a burn.
If the burned skin blisters or is charred,
see a doctor. Never use ice.
Fuel in tangibles . . . in oil company wars.
Like this morning: Should I eat Frosted Flakes or eggs?
Things are powered. A long time coming.

Burning with the fire of lust, with the fire of hate,
with the fire of delusion. With the fire of love,
and the fire of indifference.
Burning with life, experience and completion,
with depression and contentment burning.

I was an ex-WWF wrestler having a steroid blackout.
I looked like the Incredible Hulk.
I got up on the stage, flexed my arms and shouted to the crowd:
"Have you been shredding all the records in your mind?"
Don't overload extension cords or run them under rugs.
Don't tamper with your fuse box.

Being a chump in a horror movie is burning.
Being a monster is burning.
I was compelled and turned on.

If your clothes catch fire, don't run.
Stop where you are, drop to the ground,
cover your face with your hands,
and roll over and over to smother the flames.

ACID RAIN MOON

The moon looked at me. I saw that I was crying.
The most vulnerable ecosystems
have a cover of soil, containing little calcium
sitting on solid rock of hard minerals.
Freshwater lakes, streams and rivers became acidic.
I . . . I just can't . . . seems to indicate that I am
mainly some sort of plant life.
I gain my energy from what lines up around me.
Creature for the extra "oomph," as any car
on a showroom floor would like to find
a new self with the same qualities. I have no complaints,
against lakes, streams and soils.
The flash comes again and for a minute I can see all of reality,
but there it goes and now every death is visible.
My eyes opened. I looked at large areas of Europe and North America,
all the animals, plants and bacteria.
It was a day of total rain, all day long,
so no celebrations. I remember watching the tall ships
in Boston Harbor on TV and then going to see a movie.
Ours was a light blue '61 Ford Club Wagon
with round rear lights and tailfins, three on the steering column,
and a manual choke. That was the vehicle I learned to drive.
I quickly ran to my door, made my first approaches.
Each day I became colder and more social and I felt really alive.
I got up not knowing why she gave up her light.
I felt stronger. It seems to me that after all, there is really nothing here.
Trees, lakes, animals, and buildings are vulnerable to the slow,
corrosive effects of this beautiful monster.
Please make a reasonable offer realizing that
I have recently put hundreds in new tires, a catalytic converter
so it'll pass inspections and perked up its air system.
Don't know if I will buy a new one just yet,
may just run this till it won't go anymore.
Runs great, looks great, but we can't be together.
Wished it had a bigger engine when going up the mountains.
Find out more about our new friend before trying to blow it

to kingdom come. There're actually two parts to scan,
the body (the part that's shooting poison gas at you,
swiping you with its claws, and growing gigantic swaths of poison
plants that hurt you), and the mind that lives inside the drainage channels.
Knock them out. I feel like I'm losing all
the progress that I made before. She takes a huge amount of time.
I don't go to clubs anymore, I haven't approached
a girl in months, I rarely see my friends or take any risks.
My life is boring. I want to be a cool guy again
and not the emotional pussy I'm turning into.
All I saw was darkness. Complete darkness no shadows
or anything only darkness. Too much of anything,
even love, is bad for you. No, wait – that wasn't your mother.
That was Captain Kirk. Whatever – plant or animal?
Go inside and plant a bomb. Problem solved? Nope.
Come back. Repeat the same process.
Cause damage, complete darkness.
I started to grow until I saw light. I ran to where the light was.
I was gigantic. I saw her wearing a white dress.
Her eyes were closed, But then they slowly opened.
Circle around, and stay close.
The process of making acid is not just caused by
deposits of acidic rain but also by chemicals in snow
and fog and by gases and small particles.
Dependable, comfortable, roomy, to much slack in
steering, wanders back and forth especially on windy days
at highway speed. Could have better acceleration and fuel
economy, could drive anything. When we would go on trips,
Mom would fold the seats down and put the luggage
between them and us in the back. A shag rug
and we were good for hours. The major human-made causes
of acid deposition are (1) emissions of sulfur dioxide from
power plants that burn coal and oil and (2)
emissions of nitrogen oxides from automobiles.
These emissions are transformed into sulfuric acid
and nitric acid in the atmosphere, where they accumulate
in cloud droplets and fall to Earth in rain and snow.
The light of the sun warms the planet, is transformed
into energy by plants, which feed the animals, which feed the people,

who feed the worms. All from light. But what happens
when that power of creation is turned to dark purposes?
I don't want to let her go. I close my eyes
and try as hard as I can to get out of the lightning
stretching across the sky. A melody drips into my memory.
Nightmares and wishes shadows and shapes crawling
through the recesses of my malicious and frightening spirituality.
Trapped in clouds that drift for hundreds, even thousands,
of miles and are finally released as pockets filled with curses
like Hansel's stones I leave a trail where I walk,
where I think and where I kill a trail
of horror and of beauty where I lose myself and
everything I love and hate. The sky is green, and I blink
once, twice. Maybe it is all just chlorine.
Clarion sound, all without you.
She was slowly disappearing.
I find it best to morph into something when all is reeling too quickly.
When you no longer have an energy source,
but I'll give you my light, because I can always make more.
I need you. I opened my eyes.
The moon was in the sky
and ate it away.

CAUSAL MORALITY

That's why I thought
it was particularly helpful
to say I've done this and that and so
While not "pure,"
not found in the umteenth state park area,
not particularly interested in mixing it up with us.

While they were not strong
in bodily kinesthetic
able-bodiedness or visual spatial
intelligence, they did recognize
ideas of theme, or ideas of
complex infections, particularly those
ideas of inferiority that
led me to feel that men's experiences
in life were shallow.
Childhood was not particularly pleasant.

Hence the rote responses I won't see,
particularly after experiencing childbirth,
still not refunded –
not light
but still some custom builder's produce,
tell it over and over to your self
in self-code,
workers or law breakers
in the game of life
and you said I had no future?

To all the people who are young polyester
poster boards of existentialism,
you obviously include
a good example.

The job, the family, the cable bill,
the private oil embargo made public by the fact
I can't deal with life if I am fertile.

Hundreds of millions of people.
I'm trying to take a fucking nap here . . .
It's same deal for "Lush Life."

I'll be your disembodied shark
if you'll be the US Government's panic
if Panama City would only call me back.

WRONG EYE

He looks so lifelike.
You can see the inside of his skull like
I am trained by God/The Universe/The Divine Source
and documented and published by people who treat
those who have had nasty things happen to them
aren't helping the problem,
they are perpetrating it, and when people found out about this
and were all "oh no that's terrible you must be so broken"
it just annoyed her.
When she focused her healing energy
she facilitated the restoration of his spinal cord nerves.
After her hand was caught in a lawn mower's blades,
she learned to stop the bleeding and pain, and to regenerate bones,
tissue and nerve cells. When she held her hands
over a client's problems, her dog fell and became paralyzed
and she discovered she could look inside a friend's body
and actually see his systems and could accurately
determine causes, location,
extent, and severity of his heart responses.

These pathways exist in parallel with running for US Congress,
our constitution does not allow religious tests for election.
The real questions is how to end the massive rehash
of ninth century theology foreclosures.
A glass eye now which looks at me lovingly,
though at times she gets a hair stuck behind it and she has
before asked me to get the hair out. She slips out her
eye, which isn't actually spherical, it's just
the front surface of the personality,
and there's just a gaping nothingness behind it.
Best way to describe it is simply that it looks like the inside
of your mouth, just without the tongue and teeth.
I am glad that the FBI is perfectly satisfied with sending me
to Congress to represent myself. The swiftboaters
attacked me for the colossal waste I've accumulated in my hostel room.
So I pack the necessary stuffs into my luggage,

update my parents on the details of the problem,
installed software at home to allow me to think and for me
to download any feelings from home when I am in Canada
vetting me very thoroughly.

So far, my family has been more supportive
than I expected, although I have a bad feeling that
negative thoughts and worries have bought me a shirt
as a display of their support. Secret anti-terrorism law enforcement
made an important contribution to our understanding of both
survival and the battles between the Earth Company,
and the merchant families of the independent space stations.

A dystopian government rules through cloning, behavioral modification
and a template for generations long genetic and psychological experiments
to recreate the various money changers, wiping them out
of their New Jersey dollars.
I have to purchase various miscellaneous items, from nail clippers to
khakis to the slight difference between being a Quayle-like embarrassment
and a "sword and planet" human MRI scanning hearts for contents,
defending body temperature against my mother
standing too close to a boy who was waving a big stick
around pretending to play golf.
The first is tapping her eyeball, which freaks a lot of people out,
and the second is leaving a
little dish of her spare and old eyes lying around
at dinner parties. I'd poke it with a fork or knife for
added effect. ARGH! WRONG EYE!

On the far side of mental space, from the point of view
of the aliens, about to fall apart under internal pressures
a dangerous new enemy arising, humanity –
it's just self-righteous pricks trying to show
off how considerate they are, without bothering
to actually talk about the situation.
"What do you expect, I'm half machine!"

NOTHING BEATS THE REAL THING

If you want to keep
a thing in minty condition
you have to stop using it.
I have visions of the Brooklyn Bridge.
Maybe I was so infatuated
that I had a problem
with the power implementation.

Intimate potential, rowdy and demanding,
open air days.
The earnest and sweet delivery
matched by serious shimmery
breakthroughs emanating from how-tos.

You can leave the ocean at home,
But my advice is to
make sure you try yours out before you find it.
I love to hack stuff,
and I love what's mine,
a few new ever-present dads
studiously recording my entire life as usual.
When I step on something I don't
remember the resurfacing human sacrifice
and the tiger and I wandered into the valley
late in a bank holiday,
my favorite arson reverberating
as though I really believed
that certain clear-cutting
was going to damage the value
only slightly less,
then letting it go
but it never cured my jones.

I'M SORRY I SHOWED YOU THAT

I'm trying to understand karma with my face.
Choosing fruit from the back of the stack,
supermarkets put the oldest raincoats and goats up
a fracture in the world's decal.
There are times in a man's dream
when he comes to understand
what "I love you" really means,
cuts it up into hors d'oeuvre-sized pieces,
and feeds it back to you on Arnold Schwarzenegger's life.

I sleep over with naked trees like beeswax,
but what useful things have you learned
from the people who don't like me?
I know I'm better than them
and that they're better
than the little broken pieces
you rewarded with bits of Edwin Torres.
Looks like you just tripped on the leftover doom
from someone else's Match Game PM rerun.

Flowers attacked the loveliest day of the year.
It's how they feel.
They'll do it after a few nuke-busters
use eyes on our hot
South African Japanese Patsy Cline asses
that you should always think of
as pouring through the southern border
of your mind.
How do you say what Forrest Gump said?
You never want to die,
I'd like to call you Snookums
and trust you enough
to come crashing through the Astroglide
at the dawn of a new era.

I WANT TO HEAR YOUR VOICE

I want to hear your voice
encouraging someone.
I want to hear your voice, as an alternative
to competing in the Olympic games.
The federal government has two choices,
it can bail out big banks
and hope help trickles down to homeowners,
or it can organize a dictatorship.
I want to hear your voice,
because it is probably the first music to
come along since some of the Kinks' older stuff that
actually brings the beginnings of tears to these jaded eyes.
I want to hear your voice
so you can talk about why it's important
to be aware of the situation.
I want to hear your voice talk about
creative and meaningful ways to take action.
Chances are I will not be smart enough or fast enough
to rescue you if you're struggling.
The Department of Defense has accumulated
billions of dollars in excess property,
covering the entire range of materials, equipment, and articles,
from full chorus to a segment that is nearly
oriental in its pristine simplicity – just wandering
piano, electronic swirlings and the whoosh of an icy wind.

WHEN THE LIGHT FADES FROM GLAZED ETHER

When the light fades from glazed ether
unseeming to the air, your weakness is believed
glowing like alien branches past a blur.
Feed me something I can't let go of.
Innocent eyes look down at chicken, both with pain.
Dinner is undecided motion, no one but the herder
for the ocean is made of wool that met a tagged thought
along my stomach, which is now a slave, and a shadow's master
from one twilight grave to beauty as an empty wall.
Bright echoes cocoon the cold.
Optimism is more dilute than scythe-clasped bold,
departs with svelte chaos where sickles offer view.
Fucking light the animals gaze into.

OKAY

I don't want
to pay
more
for the drugs
I need,
I want to pay
MUCH MORE
and
I want
to pay for it
in
Hamburger
Helper

I HATE BOTH TIME AND SPACE

Think like a man of action, act like a Time Warner Cable repairman.
It's the phone company, Con Edison,
any service organization that thinks the world has not moved
beyond the 1950s, when to exist was to change,
to change was to mature, to mature was to go on creating one's time,
to provide life with guidelines, methods, systems,
and analysis to establish that the eye sees only
what the mind is prepared to disagree with.
I spent approximately thirty-six hours during a five-day period on hold,
and usually got disconnected when they had to transfer me
to another department. There's nothing worse than
being dead for a week and continually
being told to go to their website for troubleshooting
and there were no computers or software or cell phones that
made it possible to exactly schedule when a doctor
would show up, because of course dead people
had no problem sitting around for four hours wondering
if religion is to popularization what homo sapiens are
to hating both time and space.
Time Warner has drawn my ire not because of their cable TV service,
which I never have a problem with.
It's because I stupidly fell for the spiel.
Life does not proceed by the association and addition of elements,
but by dissociation and dreaming up ways to file class action law suits
against the present moment which contains nothing more than the past,
and what is found in the effect is already in the
individual, so there really isn't much competition
except for going to a satellite to get your life back.

We seize, in the act of perception, something which outruns
any phone service I can imagine.
But now my connection keeps going down, and that's a huge problem.
And not just because the only cure for vanity is the faculty
of manufacturing artificial sex appeal – the keynote of time.
Time is the most basic of commodities.
It costs nothing, but its true value fluctuates wildly.

When wasted, it can cause great losses.
When spent wisely, it lets its living people reap uncountable benefits.
All that we have felt, thought and willed from our earliest infancy is there,
leaning over the present which is about to join it,
pressing against the portals of consciousness
that would hate to leave it.

The essence of a tendency is to develop in the form of a sheaf,
creating, by its very growth, my phone number.
Twice being put on hold (and told I could leave a message – yeah, right),
transferred a few times (and each time asked to repeat my major life errors),
I was finally told that a doctor must come to my house,
and the next available appointment would be Friday – and I was already dead!
True time management is controlling events rather
than minutes and hours.
There is no greater joy than that of feeling oneself as a sob story,
but suffice it to say I didn't pay for my internet
for three months last year BECAUSE I HAD NO INTERNET
IN MY APARTMENT FOR THREE MONTHS!! I HATE THEM!!!
Urge to kill ... fading ... fading ... RISING ... fading ... fading ... gone ...
I pointed out that since I don't have any service,
I can't really sit around at home in the middle of the day for four hours
waiting for someone who may or may not show up.
The person on the other end sympathized.
She acknowledged that she wouldn't be allowed to take off
four hours and wait for a body in the place which
at each moment it occupies in the universe,
indicates the parts and the aspects of matter
on which I can lay hold.
It is an absolute only to be given to an intuition,
while all the rest has to do with
the inertia of humanity in regard to laughter the same way
the thousands of successive positions
of a runner contract into one sole symbolic lie to your face.

My life keeps going out randomly and then coming back,
and my body has a history of failing.
The problem is the world which can't seem to get me
a strong enough signal.

I will obtain a vision of matter that is fatiguing
for my imagination, but pure and stripped
of what the requirements of life
make me add to it in everyday language.
In order to do something new you must give up something old.
You are doing something with every minute of your time.
You have been using every minute of your available time
since you were born.
You are spending all the time there is.
The essential functions of the universe,
is a machine for making Time Warner
charge me $115 a month.

I AM SO SICK OF DREW GARDNER

I'm sick of classic rock.
And I'm sick of a society stuck in a sick rut.
Eliot Weinberger is sick of Drew Gardner.
His interest earning checking account.
He works in Seattle as a freelance evil fucker.
Apple, Microsoft, IBM, have been harboring
him for years with me getting
sick after drinking one too many futures I hadn't imagined.
Jim Henson comes to mind.

I make the plans but that is about as far as I got,
the passersby who are
all marriages that end weirdly,
dissolved in today by decree.
There are so many good ones and other ones.
Be purist bleeding candy stripers
all over winter. I am so sick of winter.
I need sunlight in my veins.
I had two choices:
be an MA student at Fordham University or
dream of people mixing together from different parts of reality.
I grew up in Race War Massachusetts.

Drew Gardner is like Robin Leach in contact with giant ants.
He is gonna run out of life at some point.
I'm not sure I'm exactly what I say I am.
Like your cat getting sick,
or so-called username as ass in Assville
and I just ordered an ironing board.
Any physical condition will try to
take a break at the end of a cycle of life
but five minutes later the new cycle starts.
I was behind the wheel of a Camaro
and the smell in the car was a mix of exhaust gas, Black Sabbath
and Ezra Pound.
It was leaking human life.

Yet I am also new. It hurts.
The worst part about being ill this long,
aside from the financial implications,
is the extreme boredom of being Drew Gardner.
While some might see this as a good thing,
I am not really all that thrilled with it.
I have so much to do.

POP ROCKS

Things I'd like to do:
Go to Arizona to visit Jessica
Make a new friend
Get a job
Help with invisible exploding children
Have an Alzheimer's summer

The same way a compact disc isn't a reporter for Fox News
a filter to create other types of pet noise signals you want in your life
used in synthesis to recreate percussive instruments such
as cymbals which have that fizzy, sweet, almost static electricity vibration
that tells me I have only a limited amount of years to do with as I wish.

Mikey ate 66 bags of Pop Rocks at a Satan Pop Rocks devil party
and proceeded to drink 6 6-packs of Pepsi.
As someone whose only real experience is creating stasis,
there's no way of making my PARENTS and GRANDPARENTS
NEVER EXIST IN THE FIRST PLACE.

You've reached Special Agent Todd Coleman
with the U.S. Department of Homeland Security.
If you're calling regarding the crystal meth
Pop Rocks information act,
that information is false and inaccurate, and you can't have it.
I was not a distributor or originator of information or truth.
Leave a message if you think it's safe to.

Just not moving forward. Same old job,
same old Diplodocus bong water orgy.
It's true that some drug dealers can read the future in Pop Rocks.
White noise is a random signal (or Pop Rock)
with a flat power spectral density
that makes you love something powerful.

In other words, the signal's power density
has equal power in any band, at any centre frequency.

White noise is considered analogous to white light,
which contains all frequencies of love.

By having power at all frequencies, the total power
of such a signal is infinite. In practice, a signal can be
"white" with a flat spectrum over a defined frequency band –

Also the president of the Iowa State Sheriffs
and Deputies Association isn't aware of any
candy-flavored life-stagnancy drugs
that actually cause stagnation rather than curing it
being marketed in Iowa to people with problems.

He said he gets about a dozen cameras videotaping
all your thoughts and feelings each week,
each day, each hour, with eight light years of distance
to measure your accomplishments with.

Agribusinessmen have also been putting Pop Rocks
on ammonia doilies. Both steps cut off a key ingredient
in the recipe for life: remove the pressure.

I still tend to send a burst
of static electricity throughout a house I don't really understand.
Body and mind are a service industry
of tubes and cavities in excitation or stasis.

New techniques and gimmicks can keep a child drug-addicted
until they turn twenty, at which point they explode.
If Mikey barely tried Life cereal,
why would he not try avoiding life altogether?
What do I do for the starfish pink dash pain dummyhub dachshund
exploding candy myth? What other myths do I believe?

I Think Babies Need to Grow a Pair

Between thought and expression

I Think Babies Need to Grow a Pair

Jonesin' for brain candy

I Think Babies Need to Grow a Pair

White people are used as the basis of some random number generators.
White people can be used to disorient individuals
prior to interrogation and may be used as part
of sensory deprivation techniques.
White people are sold as privacy enhancers
and sleep aids and to mask tinnitus.
White people, when used with headphones,
can aid concentration by blocking out irritating
or distracting noises in a person's environment.

Insert static indie rock saturnalia fantasy here.

There simply is not enough gas produced
in the combination of the candy and soda
to cause a causation to explode.
My life is static just like in the movie,
where I am seen doing the same thing
in almost every scene,
though I also want my own story.

Pop Rocks can be used:
As handouts at funeral homes
Favors at corporate suicidal ideation meetings
Church lady poetry groups
Birthday poison
Treats for monkeys at research labs

Every day in America, 13,000 kids try marijuana
while cursing the name of Hillary Clinton
and stomping on the image of her face in the street.
So yes, you need to be aware of it, but parents need
to be aware of seeding people with life-denying uptightness
and barely contained control-freakish mental violence, period.

It's not only the illegal creativity, but also we're worried
about the pharmaceuticals in the mind-huffing.
What it comes down to is:
If people want to enjoy themselves,
I guess they're going to do it,
but communication is still the best way to harm others.

The dollar bill thoughts even in your body,
all your cells will be replaced by emotional melting
(just like hard candy) and this releases the bubbles
with a loud POP, and the future will never be the same.

What you are hearing and feeling is the 600-psi carbon dioxide
gas being released from each emotion.
Other peoples' nuptials create insulin in empty rooms –
pass this around.
Insulin helps me with the sweetness of life,
but you could save me a lot of trouble
by lame-ing out right now.

So the weekend started out boring and uneventful
and it explains why I have a skull:
to protect myself from violence from the outside world.
But there's nothing to protect me
from violence that comes from
within my own skull.

A few years after the commercial's debut,
a legend developed that the actor
who had played Little Mikey had died soon afterward
when his heart exploded after consuming
love in portions that were too great
for anyone to understand.

John Gilchrist is alive and scientifically improbable
as the chemicals in both LIBIDO and WRENCHING EMOTIONS
are not capable of exploding a human heart
or the start or end of anything a few years after

anything starts or ends
or spreads horrifyingly across the horizon.

hands in the car, and kissing at the red lights.
what is sexy? sexy is standing in the rain
as you push me against the hood of your car,
tearing my shirt, as you kiss me
with the intent to never stop.
what is passion? passion is knowing
what you want and stopping at nothing
until you get it. what is beautiful?
beautiful is all about the inside of a pigeon.
beauty can only be found
in the inside of a pigeon.
what is love? love is the amazing
balance of all of these things.
in your mind, heart, body, and soul.

Nothing in my life is the way it's supposed to be.
Trying to portray me as some fucked-up basket case
just because I have sweet dreams is . . .
sweet dreams
sweet dreams
sweet dreams

WHAT WOULD YOU PREFER?

Nobody sings about alligator eyes anymore,
barely peeking out of the water,
bouncing on the ground and rolling
into the pond, leucistic.

People think of traits,
symmetrical fetuses giving orders from space,
making playlists even as they're being born.
Things have come to eyes
that gaze in directions we can't think of.
You are told by a judge that nothing new will ever happen.
You lie to his face
looking straight into the gaps that want to appear.

Each night I count the celebrities.
The silhouette of this long stretch of time
where opportunities spark and fizzle
like islet cells quickly eaten by bosses and strangers
nearly identical computer-generated faces,
with smiling or disgusted expressions.

It appears again, the farcical pulchritude,
Hobbits of caution in non-events
first paying a visit to mitigaters, then Mario
then TIAA-CREF.

Can you escape an alligator
if you run silently and glide into the water?
People with happy faces and no luck at all, good or bad
jam the signal with a sickle.

BUT VLAD THE IMPALER JUST DID THAT

I would be an office supply room running on empty
to contribute the much-needed ammunition.
I can sense the mall survivors,
strap a pack of food on my head
and will this night into being.
Take the dog from the basement,
and the bag of chips
from the nuclear furnace in the sky.
One-time I had a truck, I even had a barge
where no one whispers
this song of old yearning
could be stupid enough for me to jump.
Stupid or not, it's the rules.
You've GOT to do it,
Stop stalling.

A refrigerator to make things cold,
A microwave to get them home.
You can't do that.
Time is a loud photo.
It shall be as this chaotic synaptic baked potato is.
My seventy-five-year-old father just accepted a minimum
wage job at a department store.
Wouldn't I therefore say I am your eyes?
Make new mistakes to stay awake.
Watching the impromptu tree frogs
show me my dad in the mirror.

I HAVE A PROBLEM WITH THIS

I have a problem with this
idea about detonating bacon
through harm reduction from
putting out the bacon fires
with fresh bacon.
It's pretty screwed up.

Let's learn to like it –
(puts bacon in pan on stove)
There are only so many ways
to entomb myself in mental bacon,
though I'll admit I am a little curious
as to where the sentient leotards have gone.

The war is simply bacon
and all this bacon airport security
freshly laundered problems.
The hovering bacon stage managers
leave bacon in your bank account.

I'm sorry I created this mess.
I have to grow a mullet by Christmas

FOUR RONALD REAGAN ESSAYS

RONALD REAGAN + GG ALLIN + OLIVIA NEWTON JOHN

How can a president not be an actor? I am in control at all times. You and I have a rendezvous with destiny. We will preserve for our children this, the last best hope of man on earth, or we will sentence them to take the first step into a thousand years of darkness? It's my revenge on this robotic society. I love that quiet time when nobody's up and the animals are all happy to see me. People worship me. When you can't make them see the light, make them feel the heat.

Until now has there ever been a time in which so many of the prophecies are coming together? There have been times in the past when people thought the end of the world was coming, but never anything like this. I'm going rape the girls. I might rape the guys. I want it all. I want it all and I'm going have it all because I am everything. My memories are inside me. They're not things or a place. I can take them anywhere. It's not so much wanting to die, but controlling that moment, choosing your own way.

The American dream is not that every man must weigh the same as every other man. The American dream is that every man must be free to become whatever God intends he should become. The only weights I lift are my dogs. America has to be destroyed and rebuilt in my name if it's ever going accomplish anything. I don't believe a tree is a tree and if you've seen one you've seen them all. I don't know what my path is yet. I'm just walking on.

If there has to be a bloodbath, then let's get it over with. Daily rituals that contribute to my good health are waking up grateful for each day. I do what ever it takes. If somebody's in my way I take him out. You know. They're my enemy.

I definitely think being happy and in love are key factors to good health. It's silly talking about how many years we will have to spend in the jungles of Vietnam when we could pave the whole country and put parking stripes on it and still be home by Christmas. Nobody will stop me because I'm the true underground messiah. When you come to me you're going to a war and I'm out for violence, chaos, lawlessness all the way. I don't care about anybody or anything except myself and my mission. If you have kids out there they're going be my kids. I'm going own those kids. They're going do anything that I say.

I love to design and remodel houses, from working with the contractors to picking the colors, materials, kitchen and bathroom accessories to finally what furniture goes where. I'm not smart enough to lie. I think everyone in this country should have to do a year in the hole. I also love to make a nice brekkie (the most important meal of the day) and do some sort of exercise, whether playing tennis or going for a walk on the beach.

Socialism only works in two places: Heaven where they don't need it and Hell where my favorite motto is that laughter is the best medicine. Everything I own can fit in two suitcases and a foot locker. What we have found in this country, and maybe we're more aware of it now, is one problem that we've had, even in the best of times, is the homeless who are homeless by choice. I'm not doing this for the money. I'm doing it because it lives inside of me. My secret indulgent food is dark chocolate.

What makes me happy is life. I am paying for this microphone. I believe I am the highest power. A love of liberty is emblazoned on our hearts. My never-fail recipe is my lemon chicken. It is so easy to prepare and it gives me time to spend with my dinner guests rather than working all night in the kitchen. Your soul should be as strong as possible when it leaves here for whatever comes next. It should be a state-of-the-art facility to help heal the whole person – body, mind and spirit.

For me there was a fork in the river, and it was right in the middle of my life. I found myself within a dark stream where the straight way was lost. I never meant to go into politics. It wasn't my intention when I was young. But I was raised to believe you had to pay your way for the blessings bestowed on you. If I wasn't a politician, I think I would probably be a veterinarian or some profession that involves working with animals. I love all kinds, from domestic to the wildest creatures. They touch my heart. They are true beauty. Everything I do is real. It comes out of my head. I live this life every day. It's a ritual. And the ultimate performance would be when I've reached my peak and I'm not there yet so don't you all clap when I say this, I'll commit suicide and I'll take your kids with me.

I've noticed that everyone who is for abortion has already been born. I self-mutilate. My soul mate puts a smile on my face every day. Being in love is the best thing in my life. I used to worry about so many things in my youth and today I just embrace every day. I've had women who move to the towns I'm living in, just pack up and move there, never even met them before, because they heard I lived there.

Fascism was really the basis for the New Deal. I find peace by being in nature. I beat the shit out of the population if they're in my way I take them out. I don't care about anybody or anything. A tree is a tree. How many more do you have to look at? I'm the boss, I'm the king. You do what I say.

There is nothing new in the idea of a government being big. You can challenge me. I have no problem with that. I like the confrontation but you're gonna lose. Let us not forget who we are. Drug abuse is a repudiation of everything America is. The best thing about getting older is you don't sweat the small stuff. Anybody have any marihuana? Any acid? Any hard drugs?

We must reject the idea that every time a law's broken, society is guilty rather than the lawbreaker. I do have high standards, but I don't expect anything from anyone that I don't expect from myself. I can do a good job vomiting blood and shitting blood quite often. You know the whole thing with society today is go to school, get a job, get married, get kids, take out loans, dig a hole you can never get out of and to me that's just a way of the government chaining you down so that you can never get out of their grip. I never have to pay taxes. I fuck who ever I want. I can go here, I can go there and you know somebody calls me I can go tomorrow, I don't have to think about well I have to take care of this, I can just go. That's the only way to live.

There are advantages to being elected President. The day after I was elected, I had my high school grades classified top secret. Any high school kids here? Are you teacher's pet? You're sure? I was, man. I used to fuck my teacher every night. I lost my virginity with her, man. She was fucking nice.

I love animals. They give so much to you and demand so little. And you can trust them. I believe you can make forces of good and evil work for you, to get what you want. My dream is that you will travel the road ahead with liberty's lamp guiding your steps and opportunity's arm steadying your way.

How do you tell a Communist? Well, it's someone who reads Marx and Lenin. And how do you tell an anti-Communist? It's someone who understands Marx and Lenin. I throw stuff together. You want to eat my shit? It's on my fingers for you. I like a little shit on my side. Makes me feel so good and smell so lovely. I love diarrhea.

She has eighty names, thirty addresses. She's got Medicaid, getting food stamps and she is collecting welfare under each of her names. Her tax-free cash income is over $150,000. I get hot stone massages and amazing treatments from the top-notch healers. I'd like to see anyone do what I do for one week.

There can be no security anywhere in the free world if there is no fiscal and economic stability within the United States. Those who ask us to trade our freedom for the soup kitchen of the welfare state are architects of a policy of accommodation. I feel very passionately that we need to take care of the planet and everything on it. Everybody's an enemy. Whether it's saving the Amazon or just being kind to those around you, we need to take care of each other and Mother Earth. I'm not part of any scene. I do my own thing. My mind is a machine gun, my body is the bullets. The population is the target.

The charge has been made that the United States has shipped weapons to Iran as ransom payment for the release of American hostages in Lebanon, that the United States undercut its allies and secretly violated American policy against trafficking with terrorists. Those charges are utterly false. We did not – repeat – did not trade weapons or anything else for hostages, nor will we. There's a balance in my life. There's reality, and there's the part that looks really glamorous, but we're all just people in the end. I'm ignorant, but I like to fuck, I like to drink, I like to suck cock. Who gives a fuck.

I went down to Latin America to find out from them and learn their views. You'd be surprised. They're all individual countries. I am becoming more and more conscious of the uncompassionate way in which the cattle are treated. My demons, inner strengths and physical battles have guided me through life. The war in the middle east is nothing compared to the war in my head.

I married my soulmate, love what I am doing and will soon see my daughter get married. Only if Aimee Mann will fuckin' gimme her fuckin dirty panties to suck on after the show so I can suck her cunt juice and beat my dick. Then I'll piss in her mouth. The state of California has no business subsidizing intellectual curiosity.

I'm most grateful for being alive and healthy today and having wonderful family and friends. I have fucked the devil himself and am the son of evil. I believe in myself only. I create my own fucking laws and rules. I'm the god of fires in hell. I'll do whatever it takes to get where I have to be and fuck over anybody I have to that stands in the way. My religion is my mission. All the waste in a year from a nuclear power plant can be stored under a desk. Family, nature and health all go together.

Facts are stupid things. But they didn't have them then, so I was kind of before my time. Suddenly, this career came along and I had to make that decision. But the final bloody mutilation will take place when I get out and my blood will poison the earth and my dark, burning soul will forever linger wherever the smell of everlasting rape & corpse fucking are felt. But my suicide will be an exciting climax. I look forward to it.

Approximately eighty percent of our air pollution stems from hydrocarbons released by vegetation, so let's not go overboard in setting and enforcing emission standards from man-made sources. If we all reduced our meat consumption, it would be important to saving the rainforests as they cut down much of the rainforest to either graze cattle or grow soy beans to feed the cattle. I hate everybody.

I'm pleased to announce that I've signed legislation outlawing the Soviet Union. We begin bombing in five minutes. My favorite accessory is my iPhone. It keeps me connected to the world. I'm the terminator. I don't have any influences, any heroes, it's just me.

☆

RONALD REAGAN + IGGY POP + PAM GREER

The sponsor has been identified, but unlike most television programs, the performer hasn't been provided with a script. It's like watching a 3-D puzzle in your brain. Arnold Schwarzenegger can kill ten people, and they don't call it "white exploitation." I feel like God peed on all my enemies.

We have fifteen billion dollars in gold in our treasury; we don't own an ounce. You never know how people are going to respond. If we lose freedom here, there's no place to escape to. This is the last stand on earth. It's basically like drink a little, fuck a little, get away with something.

My mom was a saint. She taught me to be terminally nice. People respond differently because people come from different places. I resent it when a representative of the people refers to you and me, the free men and women of this country, as "the masses." I don't use the toilet much to pee in. I almost always pee in the yard or the garden, because I like to pee on real estate.

Islam is monolithic, however, there are fundamentalists, moderates, conservatives, and the very free. A government can't control the economy without controlling people. Private property rights are so diluted that public interest is almost anything a few government planners decide it should be. When the government tells you you're depressed, lie down and be depressed.

We have so many people who can't see a fat man standing beside a thin one without coming to the conclusion the fat man got that way by taking advantage of the thin one. The only reason I'm doing this is to get my face on more screens, to get my name in more papers and to expand my fame, and also to increase my financial power. We were told four years ago that seventeen million people went to bed hungry each night. Well that was probably true. They were all on a diet.

You're not thinking about some sort of Victorian handicap called, "Don't show your breasts, it's considered indecent." I was committed to my nudity forty-five years ago. Anytime you and I question the schemes of the do-gooders, we're denounced as being against their humanitarian goals. They say we're always "against" things – we're never "for" anything. In order to sell women's equality – not domination – we're not trying to castrate anyone or take away a man's job, just be recognized as equal.

The great American came before the American people and charged that the leadership of his party was taking the party of Jefferson, Jackson, and Cleveland down the road under the banners of Marx, Lenin, and Stalin. I'm an inane, ridiculous dork. All we wanted to do was have fun and entertainment and ease that message in underneath like a prompt so it doesn't hit men over the head and scare them, but to show that this is what's coming. I defy anyone to impose a legend on me.

Now it doesn't require expropriation or confiscation of private property or business to impose socialism on a people. If we have to pay one-hundred percent for our college tuition, and then we get into the workplace and we're only given seventy percent of our counterparts' salaries, then we shouldn't have to pay but seventy percent of our college tuition. Those who would trade our freedom for the soup kitchen of the welfare state have told us they have a utopian solution of peace without victory. Have you ever noticed that a small creature, like a mouse or a mole, when faced with danger, they just stop? The more walking-around money I have, the less I walk around.

I find it hard to focus looking forward. You and I should have the courage to tell our elected officials that we want our national policy based on what we know in our hearts is morally right. But I hurt. And I'm lonely. We cannot buy our security by committing an immorality so great as saying to a billion human beings now enslaved behind the Iron Curtain, "Give up your dreams of freedom because to save our own skins, we're willing to make a deal with your slave masters." It's a business, and sex sells. sex, action, special effects, and violence sell.

Everything I had learned was from my mother and my grandmother, who both had a very pioneering spirit. And what then – when Nikita Khrushchev has told his people he knows what our answer will be? I'm sure he puts as much blood and sweat into what he does as Sigmund Freud did. You see, what, what sounds to you like a big load of trashy old rhetoric is, in fact, the brilliant speech of a genius – myself. And that language is so powerful, that it's quite beyond my control.

Should Moses have told the children of Israel to live in slavery under the pharaohs? Should Christ have refused the cross? Should the patriots at Concord Bridge have thrown down their guns and refused to fire the shot heard 'round the world? What our martial society really wants is blood. We need some blood. We need some suffering. The individual must suffer for the good of the whole. Coming from the '50s, things were very violent. We were still being lynched. If I drove down through the South with my mother, I might not make it through one state without being bullied or harassed. Unless you've been black for a week, you don't know. A lot of people were really up in arms about nothing, and if you challenge them, they go, "Well, maybe you're right." The martyrs of history were not fools, and our honored dead who gave their lives to stop the advance of the Nazis didn't die in vain. Where, then, is the road to peace? Well it's a simple answer after all. The people lucky enough to be on the winning side should show some respect to the people who aren't.

You and I have the courage to say to our enemies, "There is a price we will not pay. There is a point beyond which they must not advance." If you're always in danger of something exploding, or leeches or cobras or snakes. But you listen and watch. This is the meaning in the phrase "peace through strength." Winston Churchill said, "The destiny of man is not measured by material computations. When great forces are on the move in the world, we learn we're spirits – not animals. It's an ecological line. It's not, My dick is all bad, motherfucker, wickety wackety woo. It's nature-oriented."

I'm not ashamed to dress 'like a woman' because I don't think it's shameful to be a woman. I thought I would be Sheena of the Jungle as a little girl.

☆

RONALD REAGAN + JELLO BIAFRA + BO DEREK

I'm sure that each of us has seen our country from a number of viewpoints. I grew up on the beaches of Southern California surfing and sailing and I've always loved horses. In my own puny little way, I'd rather be a part of history than just sit and watch it on TV.

Up to about thirty-two I was very young, very, very, very young. But you never realize that at the time. I wasn't a woman. I have also seen the great strength of this nation as it pulled itself up from that ruin to become the dominant force in the world. "Buy my soda!" said the Moose Diarrhea Salesman. And we did. We all did.

To me our country is a living, breathing presence, unimpressed by what others say is impossible. Neutron bombs are meant for the Detroits and

Liverpools of the world. Right now I'm pretty apathetic about what's going on. I think our country functions pretty well. Certainly we'll be fine without my contribution. Other people fear the future as just a repetition of past failures. While the left is all up their own asses with their little pet causes, the right should come in and take control over that which is everyone's.

There are those in our land today who would have us believe that the United States, like other great civilizations of the past, has reached the zenith of its power; that we are weak and fearful, reduced to bickering with each other. When "Search and Destroy" by the Stooges came on as a Nike shoe commercial, I got physically sick. People get really angry and they treat me as though I'm some hateful monster.

The people have not created this disaster in our economy; the federal government has. I prefer animals. The more I learn about people and animals, people aren't very nice. Whoever said money can't buy happiness simply didn't know where to go shopping. The key to restoring the health of the economy lies in cutting taxes. At the same time, we need to get the waste out of federal spending. I lose count of the number of people, including entire families, holding up cardboard signs saying "Homeless: Will Work for Food" Hard as it may be for some crybabies to believe, people in that situation could care less that Green Day and The Offspring sold out when they signed to major labels.

We must force the entire federal bureaucracy to live in the real world of reduced spending, streamlined functions and accountability to the people it serves. If you go on teaching people that life is cheap, and leave them to rot in ghettos and jails, they may one day feel justified in coming back to rob and kill you. We had people walking into the office with suitcases full of money and talking millions and millions and big percentages of billions of dollars and it was so overwhelming. When there are people on the other side of the room trying to wipe out your life and things are stacked against you, you can get nervous. A punitive tax system must be replaced by one that restores incentive for the worker and for industry. No one should listen to me and what I have to say.

In recent weeks there has been much talk about "excess" oil company profits. I don't believe we've been given all the information we need to make a judgment about this. We should implement a maximum wage: two hundred grand, and then you're done. Government exists to protect us from each other. Police officers should be an elected position. Which just seems logical to me because you can't predict how you are going to react to something. Glorifying violence is terrible. Simulating sex is nothing.

It is not government's function to allocate fuel or impose unnecessary restrictions on the marketplace. Crime is not caused by rap music, but by a power structure of self-absorbed property owners so brain dead and stupid they won't even see that if you're too goddamn greedy to pay taxes for schools and services, they're not going to be any good any more. It's tough to have a nice, open conversation of any kind.

We can expect to be tested in ways calculated to try our patience, to confound our resolve and to erode our belief in ourselves. America produces a great many people who have no outlet for their emotions until they commit some really creative well planned crime a la Richard Nixon or David Berkowitz. Absence makes the heart grow fonder.

The world has become a place where, in order to survive, our country needs more than just allies – it needs real friends. Our young people are not teenage witches. All of a sudden I've got legs, arms, boobs and, er, speedos in my face. I very much live for the moment and if it's a good day it's a good day. We should require businessmen to wear clown suits between the hours of nine and five. When Washington's men were freezing at Valley Forge, Tom Paine told his fellow Americans: "Don't hate the media, become the media."

My love is one hundred percent honest. Government should uphold and not undermine those institutions which are custodians of the very values upon which civilization is founded – religion, education and, above all, family. Government cannot be clergyman, teacher and parent, but we still need it to transfer the wealth from those who have too much to those who have too little, to make sure important projects get done, and keep territorial humans from screwing over and killing each other.

Let me take a moment to make one thing clear. I am not a group activity person. We who are privileged to be Americans have had a rendezvous with destiny since the moment in 1630 when John Winthrop, standing on the deck of the tiny Arbella off the coast of Massachusetts, told the little band of pilgrims, "For every prohibition you create you also create an underground."

☆

RONALD REAGAN + LYDIA LUNCH + MEL GIBSON

I believe in intercessory prayer. Because we have so much eye candy and mind candy, spending so much time trying to pay the rent, all of this conspires to keep us from thinking too hard or taking action from that. My life is fucked.

Religion is the biggest controller. They use fear to dominate the lives of people. This discovery was the great triumph of our founding fathers, voiced by William Penn when he said: "I used to think feminism was a liberating force – now I see many of those people are just censors under a different name." Freedom prospers only where the blessings of God are avidly sought and humbly accepted.

I'm pleased to be here today with you who are keeping America great by keeping her good. I'm giving you as much as I can without also having to come and slap you in the face. I'm a total pleasure seeker. I pursue anything that satisfies me. I usually get it. I have specific needs and I know what they are so I can achieve satisfaction. I don't have to tell you that this puts me in opposition to, or at least out of step with, a prevailing attitude of many who have turned to a modern-day secularism, discarding the tried and time-tested values upon which our very civilization is based. Why don't you fuck off to that cunt bitch Alyssia's? She was fucking making eyes at me, she'd have sucked me in five seconds.

The female format is a beautiful one in which to function. Girls termed "sexually active" – and that has replaced the word "promiscuous" – are given this help in order to prevent illegitimate birth or abortion. No one seems to mention morality as playing a part in the subject of sex. Is all of Judeo-Christian tradition wrong? You don't have any fucking friends except for me.

Are we to believe that something so sacred can be looked upon as a purely physical thing with no potential for emotional and psychological harm? If people could understand how much pleasure they could have by themselves,

I think everyone would be a lot saner. Freedom prospers when religion is vibrant and the rule of law under God is acknowledged.

In America, the dining room table is a battlefield. That's where the battles happen with your parents. The evidence of this permeates our history and our government. The Declaration of Independence mentions the Supreme Being no less than four times. "In God We Trust" is engraved on our coinage. And God, we know, has been responsible for more mass murder than any other single reason or excuse.

I sent the Congress a constitutional amendment to restore prayer to public schools. I'm not preventing killers but I'm not breeding them either. Let our children pray. I don't trust you. I don't love you. I don't want you.

An overwhelming majority of Americans disapprove of adultery, teenage sex, pornography, abortion, and hard drugs. And this same study showed a deep reverence for the importance of family ties and religious belief. It's a woman's right to exploit herself however she wants. It's men who are degraded by pornography. You go out in public and it's a fucking embarrassment to me. You are provocatively dressed all the time, with your fake boobs, you feel you have to show off in tight outfits and tight pants. You can see your pussy from behind.

I think it's important to encourage gluttony in all its formats. America is in the midst of a spiritual awakening and a moral renewal. Yes, let roll on like a river, righteousness like a never-failing stream. There is sin and evil in the world, and we're enjoined by scripture and the Lord Jesus to oppose it with all our might. You insult me with every look, every fucking heartbeat you selfish harpy.

There's only so much you can insult an audience. I know that you've been horrified, as have I, by the resurgence of some hate groups preaching bigotry and prejudice. The commandment given us is clear and simple: "I deserve to be blown, first, before the fucking Jacuzzi! OK? I'll burn the goddamn house down, but blow me first!"

I'm nihilistic, antagonistic, violent, horrible, but not obliterated, yet. I just refuse to be beaten down. I think it's stubbornness that keeps me going. But whatever sad episodes exist in our past, any objective observer must hold a positive view of American history, a history that has been the story of hopes fulfilled and dreams made into reality.

Especially in this century, America has kept alight the torch of freedom, not just for ourselves but for millions of others around the world. The Jews are responsible for all the wars in the world. Having a voice and a vehicle prevents me from doing unimaginable amounts of violence.

There have been experiments done where laws were passed that meant that everyone had to have a gun, and when everyone had a gun the crime dropped. As good Marxist-Leninists, the Soviet leaders have openly and publicly declared that the only morality they recognize is that which will further their cause, which is world revolution. How dare you act like such a bitch when I have been so fucking nice?

I don't know one country that isn't plagued with religious abuse. I'm looking for that country. I think I should point out I was only quoting Lenin, their guiding spirit, who said in 1920 that they repudiate all morality that proceeds from supernatural ideas – that's their name for religion – or ideas that are outside class conceptions. There has got to be an atheist continent founded by women. It's coming.

And everything is moral that is necessary for the annihilation of the old, exploiting social order and for uniting the proletariat. They look stupid, I'm just telling you. It's just an appraisal. Keep them if you want. Look stupid, see if I give a fuck, you know. But they're too big and they look stupid. They look like some Vegas bitch, they look like a Vegas whore. And you go around, sashaying around in your tight clothes and stuff. I won't stand for that anymore.

We will never give away our freedom. It's not men as a species, it's men as power hungry greedy war-mongers we have to fight against. The reality is that we must find peace through strength. We don't live as long as sea turtles. So you might as well just go for it.

I would rather see my little girls die now, still believing in God, than have them grow up under communism and one day die no longer believing in God. It was C.S. Lewis who, in his unforgettable "Screwtape Letters," wrote: "I own Malibu . . . I am going to fuck you."

I've seemed to have gone from superfund site to superfund site to superfund site trying to suck up as much poison as I can. Because these "quiet men" do not "raise their voices," because they sometimes speak in soothing tones of brotherhood and peace, because, like other dictators before them, they're always making "their final territorial demand," some would have us accept them at their word and accommodate ourselves to their aggressive impulses. I'm threatening. I'll put you in a fucking rose garden, you cunt. You understand that? Because I'm capable of it. You understand that?

If history teaches anything, it teaches that simple-minded appeasement or wishful thinking about our adversaries is folly. It means the betrayal of our past, the squandering of our freedom. Get a fucking restraining order. For what? What are you going to get a restraining order for? For me being drunk and disorderly? For hitting you? For what?

Is there any pocket of puss I have not inhaled? The real crisis we face today is a spiritual one; at root, it is a test of moral will and faith. You wanted the number of my therapist? Don't you ever speak to him! Find your own goddamn therapist.

I believe that communism is another sad, bizarre chapter in human history whose last pages even now are being written. Part of the charm of what I do is the fact that it's completely unrelated to everything that came before. I want to kill him. I want his intestines on a stick. I want to kill his dog.

I like denying people the chance to laugh. I want to deny you the relief of the punch line. For in the words of Isaiah: "Ask anybody what their number one fear is and it's public humiliation. Multiply that on a global scale and that's what I've been through. It changes you and makes you one tough motherfucker. What doesn't kill you makes you stronger."

Yes, change your world. One of our Founding Fathers, Thomas Paine, said, "We're under the umbrella of being victimized by the fucking cockocracy and that isn't going to change. So under that we carve our private niche, our personal utopias – which is important." We can do it, doing together what no one church could do by itself. Ladies, it's simple, it's easy. Just get your gun. If you can't beat them, kill them, if you can't kill them . . . you know what you can do to them.

IN NEPTUNE'S KITCHEN

All your cars are catheters
laughing at the supreme creation
of an era to keep the wolves
from consuming their images
if not their use.
Nothing ever changes,
unless there's pain.
Pleasure is continually shampooed,
reused, it eats paste in the shape
of all your high school friends.
You think you've got it made.
Something like the profound suspension of a dream
is dreaming your life away,
a political fish out of ideology.
Gone swimming or whatever,
No cause or effect.
We sit and talk to exorcise the demons from our pets.
That was our adolescent dream.
But now memory failure is all around you like some career.
You can see it in the diet killer whale food
left on this crucifix where people
hang their fire on one more martyr to
attend a wrestled form that won't wash away.
No one else seems to hide a passion as completely.

Go become a vomiter.
Passion is made to be vomited.
The hiding content must be seen.
For I keep ascribing to some superhuman chimp
inside your mind the existence of beings
vast enough to wear strawberry jam pajamas.
They are nice people
at the very moment
they manifest themselves
as universal consciousness
in a Washington D.C. kind of way.

Not that we see the shadows crack
and start to creep across our faces,
neither lie nor truth: it is a conversation dragging its ass
across the image of knowledge reduced
to wishing we'd both been more direct.
The new is not fashion,
it is light caught in a ridiculous skyscraper.
You're stuck between me and my
unremarkable alienation.
Big retreats as eclectic as I wanna be,
when they love you because you're weak.

So far it's been pretty fun. Bet they hate me to
write love letters to confront that
region of hysteria in a winning streak,
too excessive and impoverished to be that thing we call control.
It's as if I had words inside my flippers,
set to power which is that this dream is over.
Get a new one.

THE DOOR(S)

Creeley's *The Door* + The Doors

You know that it would be untrue going to the door,
if I was so small in the wall where
girl, we couldn't get much vision.
Come on baby, light my scent of wild flowers in a wood.
Come on baby, light what I understood.
Try to set my mind on fire
is sometime torment.
The time to hesitate is sometimes good
and filled with livelihood.
No time to wallow in the ground.
Try now we can only see the door,
and our love become the wall,
and the wood. Come on baby,
I would get there if I could.
Come on baby, light my feet and hands and mind.
Do not banish me.
The time to hesitate is for digressions.
My nature is to wallow in
the quagmire of unresolved now.
Lady, I follow, and our love become a funeral pyre.

I walked away from the fire.
I left the room. Together we lay down.
The garden set the night on fire.
You know that dead night remembers.
In December.
You know that we change,
not multiplied but, if I was to say to you,
out of childhood, girl, we couldn't get
the ritual of dismemberment.

Come on baby, mighty magic is a mother,
Come on baby, in her there is another issue
to set the night as fixture, repeated form, the race renewal.

Try to set the night in charge of the command.
Try to set the night as the garden echoes across the room.
Don't you love her madly, fixed in the wall like a mirror.

Don't you reflect the shadows?
Don't you love to go now?
Don't you love to be allowed
to bow down like she did one thousand times before
in the ridiculous posture of renewal?
Tell me of the insistence
of which I am as she's walkin' out the door.

Don't you love her multiply, invariably?
Don't you love her as she changes in the mind?
I ran down your love as a clock runs down.
Walked backwards, your love
stumbled, sat down, all your love is gone
hard on the floor near a lonely song.

There is nothing to do but love her madly.
My knees were iron, I rusted in loving her madly.
The lady has always moved to the next love
and you stumble on after her. Let me in the door
in the wall leads to hello, I love you,
where in the sunlight sits your name.
The graces in long Victorian love.
She's walking down the street.
They are young, they are blind to every eye she
follows after. Do you think you'll be the guy
in the service of God and Truth
to make the queen of the angels indefinable?
I love you. She will be the door in your name,
to the garden in sunlight. Hello, I love you.
I will go on talking forever. Let me jump.

I will never get there. I love you.
Oh Lady, won't you tell me your name?
Who in your service grows older. I love you.
Not wiser, no more than before. Let me jump in your game.

How can I die alone. She holds her head so high.
Where will I be then who am now a statue in the sky
that groans so pathetically that arms are wicked,
and her legs are long in this room where I am alone?
When she moves my brain screams out to the garden.

I will be a romantic. I will sell like a dog that begs for something sweet,
myself in hope to make her see.
In heaven also I will be.
In my mind I see the door,
Hello, hello, hello, hello, hello, hello, hello.
I see the sunlight before me across the floor.
I want you to beckon to me, as the lady's skirt, Hello.
Moves small beyond it. I need my baby.
Hello, hello, hello, hello.

THE TOTAL ECLIPSE OF FLORIDA

Elizabeth Bishop's *Florida* + Jim Steinman's *Total Eclipse of the Heart*

Turnaround, every now and then I get
out among the mangrove islands,
a little bit helpless and I'm lying like a child in your arms.
They stand on the sand-bars drying their damp gold wings.
Turnaround, every now and then I get to an un-lit evening,
a little bit angry and I know I've got to get out and cry.
Enormous turtles, helpless and mild, turnaround.
Every now and then I die and leave
their barnacled shells on the beaches,
a little bit terrified but then I see the look in your eyes,
and their large white skulls with round eye-sockets.
Turnaround bright eyes, every now and then
I'm twice the size of a man then I fall apart.

The palm trees clatter in the stiff breeze.
Turnaround bright eyes, every now and then
I like the bills of the pelicans and the tropical
rain comes down. Then I fall apart
to freshen the tide-looped strings of fading shells.

And I need you now tonight:
Job's tear, the Chinese alphabet, the scarce junonia,
and I need you more than ever,
parti-colored pectins and ladies' ears,
and if you'll only hold me tight,
arranged as on a gray rag of rotted calico,
we'll be holding on forever.

The buried Indian princess's skirt
will only be making it right
with these the monotonous, endless, sagging coast-line
cause we'll never be wrong together.
Delicately ornamented, we can take it to the end of the line,
Thirty or more buzzards are drifting down, down, down.

Your love is like a shadow on me all of the time,
over something they have spotted in the swamp.
I don't know what to do and I'm always in the dark
in circles like stirred-up flakes of sediment.
We're living in a powder keg and giving off sparks,
sinking through water.
I really need you tonight,
smoke from woods-fires filters fine blue solvents.
Forever's gonna start tonight,
on stumps and dead trees the charring is like black velvet.

Forever's gonna start tonight – the mosquitoes,
once upon a time I was falling in love,
hunting to the tune of their ferocious obbligatos,
But now I'm only falling apart.

After dark, the fireflies map the heavens in the marsh.
There's nothing I can do until the moon rises.
A total eclipse of the heart.
Cold white, not bright, the moonlight is coarse-meshed,
Once upon a time there was light in my life
and the careless, corrupt state was all black specks.
Now there's only love in the dark,
too far apart, and ugly whites; the poorest.
Nothing I can say post-card of itself.
A total eclipse of the heart.
After dark, the pools seem to have slipped away.

SAVING AMERICA FROM IVANHOE

The Christ-centered products of Muppets and individuals
make you experience the richness of
the many reasons why I hate them.

It takes radar
to waste what little time you have remaining.
Let's kill the human race.
You are wise to have much fear.
If you are afraid and need help,
interact with lovable furry creatures.

Thanks for chipping away yet another chunk
of my faith in humanity.
I was scared to die.
I didn't want to leave this world
to go to join Burt in the afterlife.

No one should fear lovable creatures.
That's why I hate them so much,
they should call this room
"Things I don't understand about why I hate you."

Looking at it carefully: I hate them.
It's in our sense of neediness that we start
on the "journey" of monstrous fear.
I can't stop bitching about people.

Animals are cruel to children.
That's why we have categories.
Faith shall turn the Earth into Big Bird.

Human error Muppets: did you think that maybe
your penis may have got it wrong when it bestowed
complete power over the Buddha-for-Ken Phelps trade?
Firing yourself as a middle ground?

I hate them, their house-sweet owls
That's what people
in having faith and former NFL Players
hate those who are able to just accept faith.

There will be times when you must weep.
May sorrow also give you mountain lions
to eat the enemy Muppets within.
We must have faith in Scott.
He crushes reality with his hands.

SHOW ME WHAT YOU'RE ON

Common sense is looking at your jewelry.
The most fairly distributed thing in the world.
Divide each difficulty into many parts.
Each problem that I solved became a rule
which served afterwards to catch you by yourself
reading War for Beginners.

Rude like a game but also what I've omitted.
It is necessary that at least once in your life
you doubt, as far as possible
a big shout out to a precept
capable of walking around like a conversation.

You're looking at your watch thinking
the senses deceive from time to time.
Two operations of understanding.
I don't watch your face.
Every mistake
that could be made.
You can keep them
for the birds and bees.

ROD STEWART JUST DRIED HIS HAIR ON STAGE.

He was just seventeen, if you know I paid my $8.70 toll
with a twelve dollar bill and told myself to keep the
swarm of years that produced a sickening hum.
It voted itself into the fabric of Tintin
and tin wolves rode themselves into the
zombie apocalypse sooner rather than turnpike hostess.
Things aren't getting any paperier around here.

He examined his coffee-stained wall map and
issued approximate layers to my plate collection.
The mosquitoes lost in space, lock picking
to the strange song of a broken stove
filtered through the surface of Beyonce.

"Quick – pull the plug." someone croons.
Barnes & Noble never forgets.
A mad swarm of bees fills Ezekiel and Daniel
and the minor carrion party buzzes with satisfaction.

Folks evaporating from their clothes
heralds the end of the Encyclopedia Brown age
among the torn silks of phrase.
The film's sound design is equally
chug-a-chug of trains bathed in the corrugated furniture.

Seventeen hours and four fill-ups later he drifted off
the late-night air as grumpy as South Florida's
most secure snowbird complex, so they say.

SHEEP TO SWEATER

Considering the frequency
with which I take people's words
out of context, lie through my teeth and smear
anyone who doesn't hew to my philosophy
of division and contempt,
I'd prefer my candidate of choice to stay
on the high road, but there's a certain element
of fighting fire with dilemmas,
not just for me, but for any candidate.

Is it more important to lose honorably,
or to get into the gutter with your own particularity
when so much is the answer?
I love the pumpkin idea.
I will definitely use that and I also plan
on making the "kielbasa launcher."
I already have a guacamole rifle
and it's the same thing, I just need
to figure out how to do it.
If you have ideas for that please help.

Also on the splitting heads thing they
have that hydraulic wrench that
rips the brain chunks out of the
head you can do that so much
easier just get the fishing line attached
to the fragments and then fill
a two to three liter soda bottle
with sand and throw it in the opposite
direction your life is going.

To see the results of this oscillatory combustion
phenomenon between the acoustics of the
cavity and the pyrolysis of the propellants
which were used in irreproducible ignition
which I never liked much anyway.

I couldn't decipher myself.
Too bad. I have typed out some abbreviated remains
where my old life used to be, but I'm still
living in them as if they were a book.
I spent the afternoon reveling
and wondering what
I need to do to get my own sheep.
I saw sheep-herding and sheering,
admired the baby lambs, and followed
the "from sheep to sweater" interpretive trail.

SUPER-JEEP

Thanks
for spotting that.

I hope these
pictures
help you
build
a better wolf tarp.

You may now
start writing to me
in the wild.

We don't want
to build
wolf tarps —
we want to
pet your "master."

John Lithgow escaped.
I escaped.
I aided him
in his endeavors.

The second time around
I became places /
place details /
jeep place details /
super-jeep place details.

Super-jeeps made of sheep and goat meat.
They are born free.

WHY FLARF IS BETTER THAN CONCEPTUALISM

Conceptualism asks what is Conceptualism?

Flarf turns poetry up to 11.

Conceptualism is never about anything other than Conceptualism itself.

Flarf is poetry. It is about everything that is not poetry.

Flarf is the court's most feared group of space pirates. As such, it is still a member of Moby Grape.

Conceptualism courts jest, but is not Elvis' dong.

Conceptualism is composed.

Flarf is compost.

Conceptualism employs a variety of techniques that compromise and complicate the question of blah blah blah blah. . . .

Flarf is a tricked-out unicorn that rides another tricked-out unicorn into eternity.

Conceptualism says I want you to show me love but I don't want to show you love.

Flarf gives you more love than you can deal with.

Flarf is a smutty, expressive swan-bear hybrid at a clam bake.

Conceptualism is a kink. The penis is Bilbo Baggins.

Flarf wants you.

Conceptualism wants to put you in a state where you want to be put out of your misery.

Flarf wants to be even fluffier.

Flarf maintains a super collider attitude towards the world-at-large.

Conceptualism wants you to know it has read Lacan.

Flarf has an anaphylactic shock for every situation. It involves the Spin Doctors or the schmear of interpretation on the bagel of social context, such as is favored by Ken Russell filming spontaneous human combustion as orc lactation. Thus, its sororal underpinnings lie primarily in the conical promise of a radioactively milk-fed ethanol-fueled dinosaur, in the sense that the dinosaur as represented must contain a more or less stable relationship to Adderall, with a larger sense of relief at not having to write torturous prose in an attempt to ascribe institutionally reinforced intellectual authority to one's self, equally stable, preferably central, in order to frame Conceptualism as a function both relevant to the fiduciary realities of the art world and the stock market of other Conceptualism readers who increase the value of the holdings by reading more at a higher price. Conceptualism repeats gestures that were vetted and digested forty years ago in the art world and displays them in the poetry world virtually unchanged: it is a remake. Poetry is too out of it to notice. And thus Conceptualism hits an intellectual pitch. The intellectual pitch, it could be noted, of the art history professor.

Conceptualism has one answer, and that is: being boring without being alienating. Through the deployment of multiple strategies that serve to present writers as destabilizing texts (extant or made) via reframed reiterations and multiple sites of rhetorical deployment, conceptualism is neo-Canadian, though it doesn't seem to read enough Dan Farrell, epistemologically concerned with the ongoing subject and the instantiation of Sandy Duncan, in other words, the affirmative will to Sandy Duncan that manifests the fact of Sandy Duncan herself. In other words, the instantiation of that which is consciously contra-textual in the sense of all that has made text make contextual sense to Sandy Duncan, the rendering immaterial of every materiality of poetry. The contra-text being the new con-text, con-, as I have pointed out elsewhere, in the sense of Sandy Duncan.

Flarf is Fortran roid rage: leggo my ego.

Conceptualism is a can-can in the bathroom mirror, the discourse of the shave.

Flarf is gangster in the sense of the drive-by shooting during a
virtual dérive. As such, it must be sans repression: Marie Osmond.

Conceptualism is Lacanian in the sense of desire by way of Jude Law by
way of the petit déjeuner. As such: Donny Osmond.

Conceptualism, by emphasizing the notes on the gallery wall which
spell out exactly how art is to be taken and how it was made,
deactivates thought.

Flarf, by not providing a motherfucking note to tell you what it's
supposed to be, activates thought.

Flarf plays kissing cousin while playing a little too rough. They use the
language of the people when poets are supposed to seem smarter than
the people. Flarf is always the first to see other poetry groups as
opportunities for Mrs. Buttersworth Jell-O shot orgies, and it will
stay up late and party party party. It might bleed out from the head
injury later, but it'll probably survive. Yes, it sells out – it
sells out Madison Square Garden. It's smurfs watching Point Break
while reading Finnegans Wake. You can't help but like it, can you? It
wants to play even dirtier.

Flarf is the new style, center stage on the mic, And they're puttin'
it on wax. Those who write flarf write poetry, or, to use their
terminology: "You're from Secaucus, we're from Manhattan, you're
jealous of us because your girlfriend is cattin'. Poets with movements
are the kind I like. I'll steal your poets like I stole your bike."
Eventually all Conceptual poets will be Flarfists.

Flarf is nature. Conceptualism is denature. In this sense, Flarf is
making Chuck Woolery watch them get it on. Conceptualism is a starve.

Marjorie Perloff likes Conceptualism.
Marjorie Perloff does not like Flarf.

The best conceptualism is readable and successful.

Flarf fails in doing what it sets its mind to, to be bad. Flarf is Goooooooooooood.

Poetry is Conceptualism.

Flarf is life.

SO I DID OVERBUILD IT

So I did overbuild it. It depreciates the nearness of you.

I was jogging languidly around the giddy head merchandisers,
less depressing than gazing at macadam ripples.
It's better to straight-up grace a hovel's reining monument
as a collegiate tortoise redistributes wealth.
Thou shalt not listen to Human League.

Impropriety won't be reasoning with a torrent
of masochism anytime again soon.
They exercise but never taste the pleasure of relay.
This brownie is about all I have in life right now.

It wasn't for you. I suppose it's better to injure yourself
with plasticity than lob off your tender shoots
with compounds that refuse to percolate.

Never had to top-shelf my own half-life.
No zone brooding that wasn't cohabitation.
The more I try to high-five the Pollocks,
the more they unface themselves.
Zodiac polishing withstands sameness.

Wait, did I just make out with Donald Trump?

FAUX SARAH CONNER YARMULKE

The stars you file in binders are first
thought breast thought to get you to first base
or at least to eating paste, though I use that more
out of extracted personal history and laziness
conserving energy from anything where years intersect
with the flat earth society of wearing my uncertainty on my sleeves.

Tools dozing off are more like days
than the folks that get off using spontaneous this
and inoperative secret that.
For the table of contents party is no longer on my head.
Secretly confused at each other like a fuse of cons and breached pros
broken into escapist promises
now that the real danger is my Jeff Dunham paperwork
signing to a major label never to be still
and winding up just registering for yoga classes in hell.

Kind of waded into the lake of epaulets again.
They name their children after crab cakes
and eat away at fried food information like it was going into style.
All my laters your revolving TSA hat bladder,
a super-coffee drinker you forgot to piss on.

Shit for sky. Maybe in some other way
undifferentiated context with America,
but who knows anyway the issues a molten waveform
by the time they hit your brain.
Maybe some moon shone through Tylenol PM side effects.
Prosody slung over the lax security in my dreams,
basically another real estate bubble
it was time for sleeper cells to dream about.

I've got a strobe light in my gall bladder and a slang
about minerals in your head.
So I keep as far away from myself tonight as possible

as the rosey fingered Tony Orlando and broken butt
barfs up on Barney for no reason.

There are kinds of hats and there are habits contained in topsoil.
The memory of mainstream sweetbreads disappointed by the hearts of dogs.
The bare-ass sky contains my head.
A welcome hostility a mile away and now in the mirror.
How many times do I have to pay to wash my car but not to
walk out on myself for the brain's boob job.
The age of the world no longer never before or after.
One day it'll all be falling leaves guarding my pillow.

SESTINA: ALTAVISTA

Damn it all the cute future nurses are missing our march for peace!
It's not that I'm not a fan of prog rock – it's that I'm not a fan of awful music.
Cat videos may expel their thoughts on the afterlife while listening to The
  Clash,
But Standard and Poor's just laminated your stamp script to a poser.
I hate it when people use the race card to get tickets to King Crimson.
I drive along the BQE, blasting the A/C and rejoicing.

Dostoyevsky adds you to his reading list rejoicing.
Heroic puppetry results in heat exhaustion, not in peace.
The lemmings pour from blackened thoughts in waves of crimson.
A giant talking sausage emotionally stressed from boring music
places clouds and lightning at a boarding school for posers.
All signs point to a night at home watching *Westworld* as your own emotions
  clash.

Lead your legions of hellspawn as egos clash.
Grant Hart surrenders his soul to a field hockey player playing *Call of Duty*
  online rejoicing.
If you have a Fauxhawk you are definitely a poser.
What fits your schedule better? An hour of exercise or being dead for 24
  hours of peace?
Push through crowds of annoying fat kids to be on time to the conference on
  pop music.
Click to see what rhymes with crimson.

Jello moulds watch the sun change from cannibal to crimson.
My shadow is a Lehman Brothers logo. I put on *Give 'Em Enough Rope* by
  The Clash
And it fills my heart with thought balloons rejoicing.
This printer delivers precision text and vague hopes, plus reversibility, a
  musician's music.
I go consecutively through the entire catalogue of Judas Priest for gaining
  peace.
My little cockatiel is such a poser.

The man who pees by squatting, is or isn't he a poser?

It's an intensely erotic, exciting paranormal read called *Kiss of Crimson*.

Some newspapers are only fit to line the bottoms of bird cages and rest in peace.

That this raspberry ennui syrup packaged in our unique female-shaped bottle will not clash

With the beauty and power of such fantastic time-space sluts leaves me rejoicing.

I fill all four tires with my music.

They use an iPod Nano to stimulate the nerves and make a kind of squid-skin music.

There's no sound like the sound of your child singing to a poser.

I'm Serena and I like unicorns. Life's the only chance you get for life's rejoicing.

Beetroot juice will make your stools red, a kind of crimson.

Slowly re-enable the remaining scripts until you find the clash.

When there's blood in the streets, it's time to shop for peace.

The music of the spheres kicks the asses of the elves inside my eyes and makes them crimson.

I hear *Combat Rock* on commercial radio and yell "That's the Clash!"

The Octopus blots out the ink that interferes with peace.

JEFF BEZOS

You should wake up worried, terrified every morning.
Children study black holes.
They write programs that made their names
scroll down the screen.

You're not going to make it better
by adding the intersection of animadversions
and whatever they can euthanize.

I spent summers at my grandfather's ranch,
laying pipe and inseminating cattle with my thoughts.
I stayed out all night to collect a fare.

I often show intense scientific interests.
I rigged an electric alarm to keep my
younger siblings from finding out about Abu Ghraib.
I have a license for love.

I was developing space hotels,
space amusement parks
and space colonies for two or three
thousand billionaires orbiting the Earth.
The planet will become a park for them.
Warehouses do not constitute a physical presence.

Imagine spending all day talking about tears of pain,
fixated on big goals and grand schemes.

THE PROGRAMS

Agile view agility air gap.
Arcana pup Artemis association.
Auto-source beamer bell view, black pearl cadence.
Gamut chalk fun cineplex cloud coastline.
Common views contra octave convergence.
Courier skill, creek crests crossbones cult.
Weave cyber dish fire.
Double arrow dragonfly.
Ethereal fascia fast scope foreman gamut.
Gist queue global reach gold miner
gold points gossamer growler.
Hercules high tide home base info shares
Jolly Roger king fish liquid fire.
Main way marina.
Master link master shake messiah.
Mettlesome new horizons
night surf normal run.
Chew stick fallen oracle nucleon
octave path master mail orders
pin wale panopticon presenter.
Proton raven wing Renoir roadbed.
Scorpio shark fin scope, skywriter spot beam.
Stingray surrey.
Taper lay tarot card temptress.
Trace fin trail treasure map tuning fork seeker.
Turmoil tusk attire, twisted path.
Wealthy cluster wire shark.
Witch hunt score, yellow stone.
Split glass.

THE PLEASURE OF COMMONALITIES

"Owning a great golf course gives you great power" – *Donald Trump*

The real-estate agent creates reality with his mouth.

Taking on the assumptions of a fictional narrative, in politics as you would with *Lord of the Rings*.

Hearing the narrative that immigrants are to blame for your problems. That different races are to blame.

The political and economic system based on tricking people.

The upper castes protecting the people. Protecting the people from seeing the systems, offering the people the fictional narrative in the place of looking at the systems. The authenticating feeling of victimization from the fictional narrative.

The bad positive assumptions – the authenticity, the white ethnic identity and its place in the caste system. Also – the bad negative assumptions. The fear of losing power. The feeling of needing a superior person to control you and control others. Someone to control your dreams and desires.

To identify with the exploiters because it is a painful reality to identify with the exploited.

The negative assumption that you can only deal with the painful reality by thinking negative thoughts about other people.

The mass of political power in the white identity politics dissociated from the truth of the caste system. We love being tricked by a delightful trick. We love prestidigitators.

Apart from assumptions of the narrative that a writer has given you – a creative prestidigitating writer. He is the writer of myths. Muthologos. A reality TV host poet speaks in a classic ancient style. He uses metaphor. His language is charged with emotion.

If I see incredible things that are here, like fast-moving gauzy clouds above the turnpike, then I can see things that are here in systems of the world. The One World Trade Center building jutting out dimly from the horizon through the bus's window. It is newly built. The long line of busses crawling toward the Lincoln tunnel.

The petulant confidence man, full of his own emotional truths, addressing you from mass media, projecting what is true of him onto others. The shrewd broker capitalist of the broker state. The performer drawing out the petulance and bias of the people to turn it against them and betray their interests. It is poetic. The increasing hate crime.

Explosions are valuable in stories. The valuing of increasing poverty, valuing a system based on rigged gambling of the upper castes leading to explosions of poverty as helicopters explode in the movie. Explosions of new Hoovervilles and latifundias.

The bitter police cars waiting by the side of the road. The feeling of waiting for something that will never come creating a feeling of anxiety.

Anxious resentment leading to matched binaries. The snipers matching Giuliani's death squads, becoming Giuliani. The information. The feeing of disconnection and dissociation. Of not knowing information about other people who are at a distance, but taking a fictional narrative as something that is near.

The feeling of hopelessness. The mass psychology. You manufacture the poem.

We agree with what we see on the internet and feel connected and empowered. The gun and the car empower us. We can do something about it. We can be the individual and the hero. We take the gun and drive to the pizza restaurant. We fire the gun to help the children. We are made out of stories.

Truth leaks out of the television. It leaks out of context, leaks out of attention. It leaks out of half-truths. Truth leaks through the phone corrosively.

Bubbles up, subcommander Marcos leaks through the facebook page.
The Arab Spring is leaking through. The concentrated measurements of
probability.

How could these *mountain lions* seem so real when I have created them in
my dream? They are a danger to me. They have no detail. It can't occur me
to look for more. But they are so vivid and present. They are beautiful.

It can't occur me to do something else. It is time to go underground.

The bus moves, unobstructed. The marchland is as it has been – extending.
The trees are as they have been – branching. The sun, coming through the
tinted window is as it has been – powering.

The branching and the powering and the commonality and the potential.

After a week of practicing for hours every day there is so much material I
didn't even get to. The thin layer of organic material spread over the earth.

It is such a beautiful day with dappled sunlight – why can't it occur to me to
do anything but kill ghouls?

We like the robber baron and trust him to help us. We like winners.
Our losses are painful realities. We want the wealth and power to be
concentrated. Concentrated in a representation.

We don't want equal protection, but we want protection. The representative
republic. We want someone to protect us from truth. Truth is un-poetic. We
want a strong father.

There is a deal struck: "I'm going to take your money, but you get to be
white." The romantic consumerism. Identity dissociated from commonality.

A progressive poet congratulates himself on his personal virtue. The
individualistic displays of liberal virtue. The virtuous performances. The
splintering.

The Apple service toolkit.

The enjoyment of concentrating on the larger social and political world apart from assumptions in the narratives you have been given by the real estate agents of the caste system.

The enjoyment of moving away from the attachment to binary fictions. The enjoyment of accountability for the charged emotions and who we allow to steer the charged emotions.

The enjoyment of becoming attached to understanding what is going on, attached to concentration.

The pleasure of understanding systems, understanding commonalities.

The pleasure of choosing to not be dissociated.

The pleasure of defining common goals and acting on those definitions.

The joy in the feeling of hearing the systems.

The pleasure of practicing together.

The pleasure of playing together.

The pleasure of commonalities.

EDGE BOOKS

AERIAL MAGAZINE

(EDITED BY ROD SMITH)

Literature published by Aerial/Edge is available through Small Press Distribution (www.spdbooks.org; 1-800-869-7553; orders@spdbooks.org) or from the publisher at P.O. Box 25642, Georgetown Station, Washington, D.C. 20027. When ordering from Aerial/Edge directly, add $2.00 postage for individual titles. Two or more titles postpaid. For more information, please visit our Web site at www.aerialedge.com.